# Dear Mom

---

## The Epistle From
## The Pit

---

## Adam Holbrook

### Cover By
### Holly Green

**Fairway Press**
**Lima, Ohio**

# DEAR MOM

REPRINT 2006

REPRINT 2005

FIRST EDITION
Copyright © 1994 by
Adam Holbrook

Library of Congress Catalog Card Number: 94-61560

ISBN 1-55673-965-6          PRINTED IN U.S.A.

*To Mom*
*with Love*

# Acknowledgements

First of all, I thank God who has extended His grace to me and all of mankind through his only begotten Son, Jesus, who is the Christ.

I thank my wonderful wife, Mary, who has put up with so much over the years. She deserves a medal. I also want to thank my children, Daniel, Brian, Amanda and Kellie, who have learned to love and get along with Daddy under the worst of circumstances.

Thanks to Rhonda and Bob Mowery, Brother John Miller, Dan and Judy Brady, Jim and Janice Beckett, my brother Mike, Steve H., Debbie, Pastor Steve, his wife Sharon and all the folks at Christ Chapel in Ft. Recovery, Ohio.

A special thanks to Drs. Avelina Vitug, R. J. Turner and Lonnie Herron who straightened me out after the other doctors had messed me up.

# Table Of Contents

# Introduction

Dear Mom:

I have desired many times to relate to you and the world the trials which I survived during the winter of the great midwest blizzard. I have spent many sleepless hours mentally compiling recollections of my 1978 odyssey in preparation, hoping to one day put them on paper.

The reason I have failed to do so until now is that I wanted to immortalize my thoughts as well as the facts, a task which for so long seemed to be an insurmountable obstacle.

Why? You see, the world of a schizophrenic is a bizarre combination of fact and fantasy. It is a world in which a harsh reality makes its presence known as the mind is bombarded by thoughts which are so abstract and unspeakable they beggar description.

We schizophrenics have a difficult time not only comprehending exactly what is going on around us, but also interpreting what our senses tell us. We live in an "Alice in Wonderland" world where fantasy just might be fact. It is a world in which our sight, hearing, smell, taste and touch can not be trusted. Even our most treasured memories are contorted and made to be grotesque, ugly and insidiously evil.

We not only have an often cruel reality to deal with, but we are also under constant assault by thoughts and mental images which are so sinister, so macabre, and so incredibly evil the pit of Hell itself could be their only origin.

Do you understand why I find it difficult to relate to others the strange things which dominated my thought life while I was gone? Are you able to comprehend the abysmal confusion, heartbreak and often times unrestrained terror which engulfed my being?

I pray not. Really.

I am just now beginning to fathom the full implications of the potentially dangerous situations in which I had found myself. At times I lie awake in the wee hours of the morning trembling in my bed until my joints ache because the stark reality of where I was, who I was with and the things that I did had just hit home.

If it were not for the grace of Almighty God . . .

Thanks to my best friend, savior and Lord, Jesus Christ, I have come this far. Even now, I have bad days. But I have Jesus, a lovely woman who adores me, four wonderful children, you, Bob, Rhonda and her Bob to see me through.

Isn't it odd how you always end up hurting the ones you love most? You and Bob more than any two people have borne the brunt of my illness.

But even after I broke into your house, after all the obscene telephone calls, after all the embarrassment of having a mentally ill son, after literally hundreds of dollars out of your own pockets, and even after that brutal assault on your person, you two are still in my corner cheering me on.

This, Mom, was written for you and Bob, but it is written to everyone who doesn't understand, or forgive.

I love you.

> Your son,
> Adam
> April 1994
> Coldwater, Ohio

# I
# The Departure

Dear Mom:

The day was October 3, 1977, as I recollect. It was an unseasonably warm, sunny day. The weather had been delightful for over a week.

I was staying with a friend on the corner of West Spring and South Metcalf Streets in Lima, Ohio. We were living in an ancient apartment building which no longer stands. In fact it had been condemned for over a year then.

My friend, Merle, was a sort of building superintendent who collected what rent he could from the tenants and gave it to the somewhat eccentric, elderly landlady. I was a privileged character who was allowed to stay free of charge.

The apartment house itself was a sickly green in color and housed an odd assortment of refugees from the social compost heap. You know the types. There were whores, burnedout dopers, welfare recipients plus seemingly thousands of hungry cockroaches.

You may be asking yourself how a young man of my upbringing could be living among the dregs of society. Well, Mom, you know very well how I enlisted in military service against your wishes (and my better judgment), then came close to being physically thrown out less than two years later.

You know all about my subsequent psychiatric hospitalizations. You know how I had married far beneath myself (again ignoring my better judgment) and the divorce which followed. You know very well about all of the messes and monumental errors in judgment which led me to that place at that time.

My marriage had just ended. My wife had left me and taken our only child, Daniel, with her. I knew in my heart that I was really better off without her, but I missed my son. I yearned for him and wondered what kind of young man he would grow to be without the love and guidance of a good father. That is, of course, assuming that I would have been a good father.

I had a good father. Not a natural father, but a strong father figure whom I could have looked up to, but instead hated. Had I followed his advice and example things surely would have been different for me.

He tried to teach me about life. He tried to teach me the dignity of work. I, with the exception of a few penny-ante jobs here and there, was a slothful wretch. He tried to teach me to have a mature outlook on life and about the value of money. I squandered my every dime on fleshly indulgences and the pursuit of pleasure at the expense of happiness.

I have long ago repented for those wasted dollars and years. I would put on sackcloth and sit in a pile of ashes, but such is not our custom.

At that time in my life I felt totally justified in being drunk, depressed and psychotic. Merle, may God bless his 300 pound heart, was not just a little peeved at me due to my erratic behavior. I had deliberately poured warm beer on his carpeting. I had cut his telephone line with a steak knife and just the day before had peed on his air conditioner. Through all of that, for some unknown reason he valued my friendship and did his best to cope.

On that sunny, early October day in 1977 I decided what I really needed to lift my spirits was a change of scenery, so I made plans to get out of town for a few days. What I really wanted was to run away, not realizing, of course, that it is impossible for a person to run away from him or herself.

About noon that day I walked the considerable distance from the apartment house to the Amtrak station and bought a one-way ticket on a train which was due to leave for Chicago at 5:30 the next morning.

10

That evening as Merle and a female acquaintance of his were watching Elvis Presley's last taped concert on television, I was busy packing. Actually my packing at that time was used more or less as an excuse not to join them in watching Elvis. I wasn't at all happy that the man had recently died, but I was overjoyed by the fact that he couldn't make any more records.

I couldn't sleep that night. (In those days I had much trouble falling asleep until I was near total exhaustion.) I thought getting drunk might help. Just before 1:00 a.m. I walked to a nearby pizza parlor and purchased a six-pack of beer.

Once back in the apartment I drank the six brown bottles of beer in rapid succession, but to no avail. I was fatigued and nearly in a drunken stupor but still unable to sleep.

I began to think about my life, the places I'd been, the people I had known and about my abbreviated hitch in the military.

I began to wonder, as I do to this day, exactly why it was that a few self-righteous individuals at that Air Force base took it upon themselves to drive me insane and ruin my life. Was I really that bad a person? Had I committed some heinous crime for which such treatment was justified?

I worked shoulder to shoulder with mental health professionals daily. How could they not notice that I was falling apart? Why didn't they help me? Granted, I was a boisterous, dope-smoking, foul-mouthed brat in those days, but doesn't even human decency dictate that we help those who are in need of it?

Couldn't my colleagues see that my substance and verbal abuse was only symptomatic of deeper problems? What about that cruel farce in the military they call professional ethics? Why were the words "compassion" and "brotherly kindness" meaningless and vain, as if conceived in the sick mind of a depraved, demonized jokester? As I pondered these things, the tears began to flow.

About 4:00 a.m. I woke Merle and his girlfriend up and they drove me to the train depot. Just before I boarded the train, Merle asked me to pick up some kind of souvenir for him while I was in Chicago. I promised him that I would and

11

repeatedly assured him that I would return within four days. He didn't know that I had purchased a one-way ticket.

At times I deeply regret breaking that promise I made to my friend. But, in the breaking of that promise came the opportunity of a lifetime: that is, to see and experience things which most of my peers will never see and experience.

The breaking of that promise has brought me much sorrow, heartache and even personal danger. But on the other hand, that act has brought me adventures and memories which have contributed much to the rich, full life that I now live.

I boarded the train and took a window seat. In the faint blue glow of the street light I could see Merle's portly figure waving goodbye. My eyes filled with tears. I knew it would be some time before I would see my hometown, if ever, again. I had made a decision to run away. From what I may never know. I didn't know where I was going, but I knew that I was going.

# II

# Chicago

The sun was about to peek over the yellow horizon as the train slowly ground to a stop in Ft. Wayne, Indiana. A man dressed in a white dinner jacket and black bow tie passed through each passenger car ringing a small brass bell announcing that breakfast was being served in the dining car.

I was a little hungry, so I made my way to the designated dining area and there had breakfast with a middle-aged couple who were on their second honeymoon. There was also a young man at our table, a sailor who was returning to the Great Lakes Naval Station near Chicago.

The young military man sat ramrod straight in his seat and was, for the better part of the meal, non-verbal. His uniform was neatly pressed and everything about him was picture perfect right down to the burr haircut. I grinned and chuckled to myself when I thought of how much he reminded me of a photograph I'd seen on a Navy recruiting poster.

After exchanging polite goodbyes with those at the breakfast table, I found my way back to my seat. Other passengers had boarded the train in Ft. Wayne. Among them were a 40-ish lady and her attractive, young daughter who were seated behind me.

By this time the sun was up and shining gloriously as we rolled out of the city and lumbered through the Indiana countryside. As the train rolled along, the rails rumbled beneath my feet and the constant clickity-clack had an almost hypnotic effect. I began to fantasize.

What if that lovely, young lady behind me saw the desperation, the hurt, and loneliness in my eyes? What if she perceived my pain? What would I do if she offered to sit next to me? Would I be any better to her than I had been to my estranged wife? What if she turned out to be the beautiful, loving girl that I had dreamed I would meet on this journey? What if our meeting on this train was the start of a lifelong, loving relationship? Yeah ... what if ...?

As the train neared Chicago I roused out of my daydreams and began to notice a drastic change of scenery. No longer were there quaint, agrarian villages and golden fields. There were crumbling buildings and crowded streets. There were people out there whom God loved of all sizes, shapes and colors. There were tattered garments hung on clotheslines strung between tenement buildings. There were people selling hubcaps on street corners, shouting like barkers at a carnival to passersby.

The yellow, stained sheets flapped in the breeze above the noisy, narrow, congested streets. Banners they were, reminding all of the hopelessness and helplessness which makes up life in the inner city.

As the train slowed and screeched to a stop, I found myself wondering what I would do to occupy myself in Chicago. Being in big cities always made me a little nervous because of all the horror stories about the muggers and other persons of the baser sort who lurk behind every lamppost just waiting to prey on unsuspecting country boys. I was certain of one thing, though. It felt good to be out of Lima, if only for a few days.

I stepped off the train into a very dirty, depressing terminal. The air was saturated with the stench of burning diesel fuel which seemed to press in on every side. The odor strongly resembled that of someone's funky armpit and diesel fuel mixed together. I nearly choked.

I had been told that Chicago got its name from two Indian words, Shikok-Ko, which together mean "place of the skunk." If that is so, Chicago surely lived up to its Native American name.

I claimed my suitcase and proceeded through the filth into the building itself, which was being remodeled. By then I was convinced that any change would have been an improvement.

I bought two hot dogs and a Pepsi-Cola from a tired-looking old man and sat down a bench to eat and drink. After I had finished, I checked my suitcase into a locker and tucked the key into my shoe, just in case I was to get mugged. Then I set out on foot to see the sights of Chicago. I'd been to Chicago before, but on those short trips I really hadn't seen much of the downtown area.

The first thing I noticed were the beautiful women. They were wearing the kinds of clothing you would expect to see on professional, well-paid yuppie ladies. Their hair was just gorgeous and their makeup was flawlessly applied. Everything about those girls spelled class. Pure class.

I suppose I should have kept track of the streets I walked. It is a minor miracle that I found my way back to the train depot. Another minor miracle lies in the fact that I didn't get the roof of my mouth sunburned from staring at the tops of the tall buildings with my mouth open.

It was nearly dark when I returned to the train station. To this day I don't know what made me do it (I suppose I could unjustly blame it on the devil), but I went to the ticket counter and bought a one-way ticket to Denver, Colorado.

By the time I boarded the train for Denver I was exhausted, and I slept for a time before the train left the station.

I awoke with a start as the train began to move. I felt for my wallet in my pocket, removed it and checked my money supply. I was down to a 20 dollar bill! I was frantic! I was on my way to Denver with only 20 dollars and some loose change.

I slumped back in my seat. It was too late to get off the train. My heart pounded as I stared out the window into the darkness. I thought of calling you and Bob at the first stop, but no, I couldn't do that.

"No!" I resolved. "My folks are not going to bail me out of this one!"

I swallowed hard and took a deep breath.

# III

# Denver

The ride between Chicago and Denver was unlike the first leg of my journey. The railroad cars pitched violently to and fro. My heart was in my mouth for at least 200 miles. I finally drifted into a troubled sleep. When I awoke the train was stopped in St. Louis, Missouri. "Looks as bad as Chicago," I muttered and then went back to sleep.

I really don't know how long the trip from Chicago to Denver took because I slept most of the way. I would rouse out of my slumber just long enough to catch a glimpse of a rural village on the Great Plains or when the train passed a crossing and the ding-dinging of the warning bells would graphically illustrate the Doppler effect.

I would rouse out of sleep, make certain the train was still right side up, then doze off once more. The closer I got to my destination, the more confident I became that I would arrive safely. I had my doubts about that at first.

As I stepped off the train in Denver, with suitcase in hand, the full impact of my foolhardiness hit me like a ton of fresh-baked dinner rolls. I walked into the terminal building and sat down on one of the hard wooden benches wondering what I was to do.

I was tired, hungry and nearly devoid of financial resources. I thought of going into the men's room and slashing one of my wrists. Then hopefully someone would call the paramedics who would take me to a hospital where I could at least get three hots and a cot. I hurriedly dismissed that line of reasoning. A plan such as that would require a certain degree of intestinal fortitude to carry out. At that time I was the original gutless wonder.

At length, I decided that I should take a look around outside, as the train depot was soon to be closing for the night. I gathered my belongings as well as my courage and went out as twilight was settling over Denver.

I found that the depot was at the end of a long and dismal street with decaying buildings on either side. The street was littered with broken bottles and bits of trash. I took note of the empty 55-gallon steel drums at every corner. I wondered within myself why they had been placed there.

I had walked a few blocks when I looked at a street sign, hoping to get some foggy idea of where I was. In the near darkness I could discern from the sign that I was on the corner of Seventeenth and Blake Streets.

(A man who lived in Denver recently informed me that the corner of Seventeenth and Blake no longer exists. According to his report, the Colorado Rockies now play baseball in a stadium built on that site.)

I was a frightened, small town boy all alone in a big city. I was thinking of where I would spend the night when I looked a short distance down the street and saw a red, flashing neon sign which read HOTEL. I perceived that in order to get there I would have to pass by at least two motionless bodies lying in the gutter. Whether they were dead or alive I didn't know, but I proceeded, trembling as I went.

After a short walk at a somewhat hurried pace I arrived at the hotel: the Barth Hotel. Judging from its outward appearance it could have been more aptly named the *Barf* Hotel. It was seedy to be sure, but what's that old saying, any port in the storm?

I checked into the hotel and went to my room on the third floor. My first impulse was to exclaim, "Sweet Jesus! What am I *doing* here?!"

The plaster on the walls was cracked and some of it had fallen onto the bare wooden floor. The only lighting fixture in the room was a single, low-wattage light bulb above the antiquated, badly stained porcelain sink. The only bathroom was down the hall. I joked with myself a little and mused about the availability of room service. But what could I expect for five dollars a night?

I read the obscene graffiti on the tub room walls as I bathed that night. I shaved in my room and went to bed early. My sleep that night was fitful. The old, steel-framed bed creaked and moaned under my weight as I tossed from side to side.

I awoke the next morning to a commotion on the sidewalk below my window. I sleepily arose, pulled back the faded curtains and peered down into the street. It appeared as though two vagrants were fighting over something. I watched with interest for about two minutes until the stronger prevailed. He pushed the other to the concrete and ran down the street toward the railway depot with the prize he had won in bitter combat — a half-empty bottle of cheap wine. I looked at my watch. The time was 9:58 a.m.

I dressed and went to the ground floor of the hotel. I discovered a cafe next door to the Barth, so I ate my breakfast there and then set out on foot to see what I could see.

The mid-morning sun felt warm on my face. I looked to the west and beheld the Rocky Mountains with their snow-covered peaks jutting majestically against the unclouded, blue sky. I yearned to go up there and silently promised myself that some day I would.

Within hours I had become very fond of Denver and had set my heart on staying. I filed a change of address form at a branch post office near the Barth Hotel so that my monthly disability compensation checks would be forwarded to my new home.

The next day while on a long walk I happened upon an apartment building with a For Rent sign in one of the windows. I inquired at the manager's office about the vacant apartment. He took me to the second floor and showed me one rather large room with a tile floor, an unmade bed and a sink. There was what appeared to be an antique, gas cooking stove in one corner of the room. The man gave me a rather terse speech

19

about all utilities being furnished and informed me of the bath being down the hall. It wasn't until I asked about telephone and cable television service that he cracked a smile.

I had grown accustomed to such ramshackle places of abode and the price was right. I told the manager that as soon as I got some money I would be back. I was living in a fool's paradise.

After a few days my money ran out. I checked out of the Barth Hotel with no place to lay my head.

That same day, with my suitcase at my feet, I was near tears standing under the 17th and Blake sign when two young men whom I'd never seen before approached me.

"Hey, man!" one of them shouted. "Paul's been lookin' for you. You gotta job if ya want it."

Paul was a tall, rotund man with a beard who managed the little cafe next to the Barth Hotel as well as another little diner not far away called The Hinky Dink.

To make a long story short, I landed a job washing dishes on the evening shift at The Hinky Dink. I was paid $15.00 a day in cash plus a meal. The pay was enough to get me back into the Barth Hotel plus provide me with a nightly trip to the hotel lounge. The only thing that I didn't particularly care for was walking the six blocks from work to the Barth after dark. The ragged people whom I passed on the way gave me the jitters.

For three weeks I washed dishes until eight in the evening, walked back to the Barth Hotel and got sloppy drunk in the lounge. I was beginning to love Denver and had grown accustomed to stepping over winos on my way to and from work. Actually I was no better than they were. The only difference was that I had a means of supporting myself and came at least close to being a respectable drunk. Alcoholic, I think, is the popular term.

I was working one evening at The Hinky Dink and made a joking remark about intentionally clogging up the plumbing. Paul got wind of it and I was promptly fired.

I stayed one more night at the Barth with no money to pay for the room. When the time came to pay up, the manager confiscated all of my belongings in lieu of the rent money. Literally all I had were the clothes on my back. The first of the month was close at hand. Perhaps my disability check would arrive soon.

Once again I was living in a fool's paradise. Day after miserable day I waited in the lobby of the Barth Hotel praying for the postman to deliver my government check, which never came. At night I slept where I could. Those empty steel barrels, I discovered, were for we homeless ones to kindle fires in, that we might warm ourselves on those cold, autumn nights.

In desperation one day, I decided to call Merle, collect of course. He agreed to accept the charges.

"Hello! Merle? This is Adam."

"Adam! Where are you? I thought you'd back in four days! It's been six weeks!"

"I'm in Denver, Merle."

"Colorado?"

"Yes, *Colorado!*"

"Listen, Adam. Everybody's been lookin' for you. Your Mom . . . your brother . . . even the cops!"

"Forget all that Merle! Is my check there?"

"Your VA check?"

"*Yes*, my VA check. Is it there?"

"Is it supposed to be?"

"Oh, just forget it Merle. Just forget that I called."

"*Wait a minute!* What do I tell your Mom . . . and the cops . . . Adam?"

With that I hung up the telephone.

The next day I found a coin on the sidewalk which I used to call the police. I told the officer on the other end of the telephone line that I needed a ride to the nearest psychiatric facility. He told me that he didn't run a taxi service and hung up on me.

I hadn't bathed, shaved, nor eaten in many days. Nor did I have a change of clothing. Finally, desperate and near starvation I walked to the Continental Trailways bus depot. In the men's washroom I removed from my wallet a razor blade which I had saved for just such an occasion.

I neatly sliced the inside of my left forearm at the elbow. The wound stung and I wept bitterly as my life's blood streamed down my arm and into the sink. There were other men present, but none offered to help. After a few minutes the bleeding stopped and I was left to live.

"*Why*, God?!" My heart cried out. "*WHY*?"

I came to my senses and realized that I really didn't want to die, but I didn't really want to live either. I also came to the realization that I would face a death worse than suicide if I didn't get out of the city. I had never been a street person and didn't know the first thing about survival on the streets. I inquired at the ticket counter about the best way of getting to the freeway and started walking in that direction.

When I reached the freeway my forearm was still stinging from the razor cut. I positioned myself at the top of the on ramp.

"Well," I said to myself with a heavy sigh, "here goes."

As I stood there, holding out my right hand with the thumb extended, it suddenly dawned on me that I had never before hitchhiked. Worse yet, I had no idea of where I was going. All I knew is that I was going ... somewhere.

# IV

# On The Road

As I stood soliciting rides in the November chill I began to think of the home I'd left behind. There was always plenty of food and warmth at your house, Mom.

I called to mind those special Christmas Eves with the family sitting in the warm glow of your fireplace. The little multicolored lights on the Christmas tree and across the rough, wooden mantel would twinkle. Those tiny lights cast dancing, evergreen shadows on the faces of little Mike and Eric, my first nephews.

I remembered the Thanksgiving Days at your house. Standing there in the cold I could almost catch the scent of the golden-brown turkey fresh from the oven. I could almost taste the specially-made dressing, the dinner rolls and your special giblet gravy. I remembered how we joined hands and prayed over our meal giving thanks unto God our creator, for his blessings.

My heart was torn asunder as my empty stomach growled. Those precious moments at your house seemed to be so long ago and so far away. But you know, Mom, in that moment I realized that in those days that was my house too. I was a beloved member of the family who had turned traitor and gone whoring after the gods of this world. I wondered if I would ever be allowed back into the warmth of your love.

Lost in thought, I nearly didn't notice the baby blue Ford pickup truck stop just beyond me on the ramp. I shook myself back to reality and ran to the truck. A pretty, blonde lady leaned across the cab and opened the passenger side door.

"Where you headed for?" the lady asked as I climbed in.

"I really don't know," I said, pulling the door closed.

The pretty lady giggled. "I can't take you where you want to go if you don't tell me ..." Her voice trailed off as her bright smile faded. "Okay," she said, fixing her eyes on the road ahead.

"Where am I, anyway?" I asked.

"You are on Interstate 70 just west of Denver. Are you sure you don't know where you're goin'?"

Think fast, Adam. "Well," I choked. I cleared my throat. "I'm going to ... to ... Salt Lake City," I finally blurted out.

The pretty lady's winsome smile returned to her face. "Well, in that case you are headed in the right direction." She glanced at me, her eyes leaving the road for a second. "Say," she said, "you look kind of ragged. Why don't you let me take you home for a bath and a hot meal?"

"No," I said, taking note of her yellow gold wedding rings. "I don't think your husband would appreciate that."

Frankly, her offer frightened me. What if she were involved in a cult of some kind? If I had gone with her, I could have been sacrificed to Satan or some such evil deity. I was thinking on that when she said, "Oh, he wouldn't care. We've taken in lots of strays."

"No. That's okay," I said as calmly as I could. "You have already done enough."

"Suit yourself," she replied. She was noticeably disappointed.

We continued up the highway in silence for a few miles. Presently she stopped the truck on an exit ramp which led down a steep hill into a small hamlet, the name of which now escapes me.

"I'll be getting off here," she said as she handed me a pair of thick leather gloves. "You'll be goin' through the mountains and you sure will need these. It gets cold up there this time of year."

I thanked her as I climbed out of the truck. I watched as she drove down the hill into the Rocky Mountain sunset until the truck disappeared behind a huge pile of boulders.

24

I was next given a ride by a young hippie type in an old van. We rode in quietude for a time before he let me off at Georgetown. Before I exited the van he gave me a holey (that's holey, not holy) wool sweater which I have stored away in a cedar chest yet today. I take it out occasionally just to have a look at it when I want to remember that somber, silent young man who showed me such kindness.

In a small way that young fellow and the pretty blonde lady had brought to me a great truth. That indisputable truth is that the world is full of good people, so long as you look for the good in every person. If you look for good, you surely will find it, sometimes in the most unlikely places and in the worst of circumstances.

By the time I had reached Georgetown the temperature had dropped noticeably. I put the sweater on under my dirty suede jacket and was thinking of where I would spend the night. I stood shivering as car after car whizzed by. Each time a new pair of headlights appeared over the hill, I would extend my right thumb in expectation only to see the vehicle go by in a blur.

I was getting progressively colder and more bewildered when along came another set of headlights, these moving more slowly than the others. I extended my arm once more, hoping against hope.

To my surprise the vehicle slowed and stopped on the berm of the roadway. In the faint blue glow of the highway lights I could discern the vehicle as being an old panel truck.

As I ran to the panel truck the side doors swung open and I climbed on board. In the driver's seat was a long-haired, young man with a young lady beside him. In the back were two other hitchhikers, one of whom was sitting on a five gallon can labeled Pure Honey. The other bore a striking resemblance to Charles Manson.

"Where are you going?" asked the young driver.

"Where am I goin'? Ah, Salt Lake City! Gotta job there," I lied.

"All right," said the driver's female companion. "We can give you a ride through at least part of the mountains. You cold?"

25

"A little," I lied again. The fact was I was freezing. "I waited a long time for a ride."

"That doesn't surprise me," she said.

The Charles Manson-looking character extended an unwashed hand. "My friends call me Cherro-kee," he said.

"Nice to meet you. Ah . . . Cherokee." I shook his hand and laughed nervously. I thought to myself, "This guy is weird!" He made me nervous.

The other hitchhiker began to complain bitterly about the seat of his pants being sticky. He offered to trade places with me, an offer I graciously declined.

In the headlights of that ancient panel truck I could see snow blowing across our path. It seemed to be getting colder too. The radio of the truck was tuned in to a local station and we heard a weather report. It was 17 degrees.

After what seemed like 20 or so miles, the driver stopped the panel truck on an off ramp.

"Here's where we get off," he said.

As we three hitchhikers climbed out of the truck we thanked our host and hostess. We could see the lights of a village just below us.

"You guys wanna go down there and scout out a place to crash?" I asked, my teeth chattering.

"Naw, man," said Cherokee, pointing to his tattered backpack. "Don't need no place. Got it right here. Gotta tent, coffee pot, everything we need. Let's go up the mountain a ways."

"No!" said Sticky Pants emphatically. "I'll wait here for another ride."

"Suit yourself," said Cherokee. He beckoned to me with his hand. "C'mon."

We struck out through the darkness. The snow was about four inches deep and steadily falling. It soon filled up my shoes. Our pant legs snapped in the breeze as we sought out a suitable camp site. We soon found one near some trees which gave us some shelter from the unmerciful wind.

As Cherokee pitched the tent I built a fire. I thought about the other fires I had built in the fireplace back home. I remembered how the flames flickered as the family basked in its warm glow on many a winter's eve.

I thought about how during one November snowstorm before the house was finished we lit that fireplace and made dinner in a scoop shovel placed on the glowing embers. Home ... it might as well have been a million miles away.

The camp having been set up, I removed my soggy shoes and socks and placed them near the fire to dry and propped my feet on a log to warm them. After a little while the wind laid, making our encampment more bearable. We melted snow and made instant coffee. After we had shared the last cigarette either of us had, Cherokee looked into the darkness and said, "Well, they should be here any minute now."

"Who?" I asked.

"Any minute now there'll be a whole family comin' up this here hill." He drew a deep breath and continued, "Yep. Any minute now. And ya know what?"

"What?" I asked, growing uneasy.

"Well, they'll have a whole carton of cigarettes just for you and me. Yep, just for you and me ... the only problem is ... *They're all dead*!!!"

"Hey!" I said as my pulse quickened. "Why don't you crawl into the tent and get some shut-eye and I'll keep the fire goin'?"

"Great idea!" shouted Cherokee, slapping his knee with his dirty, right hand. "Then after a while wake me up and you can get some sleep." He pulled up the tent flap. "See ya later!" he bellowed, then disappeared into the tent.

As soon as I heard Cherokee snoring I hurriedly put on my shoes and socks. They were still wet. My heart raced as I ran back down the mountain, tripping over roots, wire and deep snow as I went. It was pitch-black. I had no idea where I was but I kept going until the sound of my heels on the pavement told me I had reached the road. I strained my eyes hoping to see oncoming headlights but there were none. My feet ached with cold as I stood shivering.

27

After three minutes or so I could discern headlights approaching through the blackness. They belonged to a semi-truck which nearly ran me down. The truck went by with air horns blasting. I cursed the driver as I fell backward into a snow bank.

I got to my feet and waited there in the darkness for what seemed like eternity before three young men in a pickup truck stopped to give me a lift. I had to ride in the back, but I was thankful for the cap which covered the truck bed and gave me shelter from the wind.

As we started into the darkness up that mountain road I took my shoes off. I frantically rubbed my numb feet fearing they had been frostbitten. I kept saying out loud, "Oh, god! My feet! Don't let me lose my feet!" With that cry on my lips I fell asleep in the back of that truck somewhere up a lonely mountain road.

# V

# The True Christian

"Hey! Hey!" said one of the young men who was in the pickup truck as he jostled me into wakefulness. I awoke and stared bleary-eyed into his face. "Ride's over. You have to get out," he said after he'd shaken me several more times.

I opened my eyes wide. The bright sun shining over Vail, Colorado, nearly blinded me. As I put my shoes back on I noticed that something strange had occurred. My feet were warm. On a ride through the frigid Colorado mountains my feet, which had before been numb with cold, had become toasty warm.

Feeling much rested I gingerly climbed out of the truck and found I was in the parking lot of a Holiday Inn.

As I breathed in the cool, clean mountain air I felt somehow exhilarated and more alive than I had ever been. I paused for a few moments and took in the natural beauty which surrounded me. I beheld the indescribable majesty of the sunlit, snow-covered mountain peaks and gazed at the frosted evergreen trees as they sparkled in the early morning sun.

It dawned on me that I was in the midst of scenes which some people would never see in their lifetime. I was going places and seeing things they would only see on postcards or calendar photographs.

With an odd sense of fulfillment, the likes of which I had never known, I walked the hundred or so yards back to the highway and took up hitchhiking once more.

By that time I had learned one important thing about hitchhiking. It takes patience. I stood by the roadside for nearly an hour and was growing a little discouraged when a man in a telephone company van stopped and gave me a ride.

"How far are you going?" asked the 50-ish driver as he looked at me over the top of his horn-rimmed bifocals.

"Salt Lake City," I replied.

I couldn't help but notice the gospel music which emanated from the radio. I listened as we meandered through the mountains, up hills and around curves for about 40 minutes.

"Are you a Christian?" I finally asked.

The driver looked startled. "Why, yes. Yes, I am," he replied.

I turned toward the window. "I used to be," I mumbled half to myself while staring absent-mindedly out of the window.

"I don't understand Christians," I continued. "In fact, I don't even really *like* Christians. But, I'd like ..."

Before I could finish the sentence the driver abruptly stopped the van. "I'm going to let you out here," he said.

Almost before I could get out and close the door, the van sped off in a cloud of dust, spraying loose gravel and snow all over me.

I stood there on the side of the road furious, flabbergasted, and disgusted. "What's with you, man?!" I screamed out loud.

I had given him my heart on a silver platter and all he could do was throw me out of his van in the wilderness. The fact was I was longing for someone to lead me back to Jesus. My heart yearned for some comforting words of wisdom and truth.

As I stood swearing by the side of that lonely stretch of highway, I hardly noticed another van approaching. I was in utter astonishment when I saw it stop just beyond me. I ran to the van.

"Need a ride?" a gentleman of about 70 years shouted out the driver's side window.

"Sure do!" I said, as my anger erupted into joy and I climbed on board.

The van was really sort of a mini-camper. It was loaded down with fishing gear and had a cot in the back.

"You like the outdoors?" I asked.

"Oh, yes," said the old gentleman. "On my way up north to do some fishing. Where might you be going, young man?"

"I don't really know for sure," I replied. For once I had told the truth.

"Just out to see the world, I'll bet," the driver said as he turned to me and smiled. "There's a lot of it out there to see, by George. A lot of it."

We rode along for a time in silence. I was impressed by his slow, unhurried, easy-going manner. He drove as if he had eternity to spend on his fishing trip. He seemed so wise and all knowing, a real sage.

The silence was making me uneasy, so I was the next to speak. "Are you married?" I asked.

"Widowed for three years this March," said the sage, glancing down at his speedometer. Then he added, "I had a good woman. Good women are hard to come by, but I had a good one. She cooked my food, cleaned my house and washed my clothes for 42 years. We had five little ones. Boy, I sure do miss her."

"What was her name?" I asked, as the man smiled.

"Margaret," he said. "But I called her Marge. Sweet little woman she was."

"Sounds like you really loved her," I said.

"Yeah," said the man, breathing a heavy sigh. "Still do," he added.

"Any grandchildren?" I asked.

"Seven," he replied. "Four boys and three girls."

"You must be awful proud of them," I said.

We drove on and talked. Every time he asked me about myself, I'd sidestep the question. I was running away from myself and the less I said the better off I seemed to be. For several hours we conversed and before either of us knew it we were in Grand Junction.

"You hungry?" the driver asked as we drove onto the parking lot of a convenience store.

"A little," I said.

31

What an understatement! The fact was that I was starved. My elderly comrade fueled up the van and went inside. He returned with a pound of bologna, a loaf of bread and a jar of mustard. He laid the groceries in my lap. I looked at them with hungry eyes.

"Go ahead," he said. "Eat all you want."

"Don't you want any?"

"No. No," he reassured me. "Go ahead." He pointed to the food. "Eat."

I must confess that I made a pig of myself. But I was so hungry!

We drove along Highway 70 until we got to Route 28 and from there headed north. As the highway hummed beneath the tires of that old van, we talked and I took in the scenery. For the first time in months I was actually laughing.

We traveled on and passed through Nephi and Provo, Utah, until at last we arrived at Salt Lake City.

"You can ride longer if you want to," said the old gentleman. "I really enjoy your company."

"No. I'll get out here," I said, shaking his callused hand. "I won't forget you."

You know, Mom, as I write this I can't help feeling that my adventure was a carefully contrived conspiracy. Like in Denver, the two young men told me of a job just when I needed one, but I blew it. Perhaps the man in the telephone company van was supposed to witness Jesus Christ to me but I spooked him.

The kindly gentleman I just told you about deliberately took me through Grand Junction, Colorado, and I was supposed to look up Fran (a girl I made friends with in the military who was from Grand Junction), but again I blew it. Later on, I passed within 20 miles of Gustine, California, the home town of Jeanette, my ex-girlfriend. Was I supposed to have looked her up? It is strange. Even now my mind tells me weird things.

# VI

# Drunk And Disorderly

It was nearly dark when I arrived on the outskirts of Salt Lake City. I got a good look at what I presumed to be the Great Salt Lake. I was standing along the busy thoroughfare taking in the view when a shabby, old pickup truck stopped and the driver beckoned to me.

He was a cowboy type, unshaven and with no teeth. As I came near he asked me if I needed a ride. I answered affirmatively and climbed into the already crowded cab. Inside were the driver, Joe, a woman named Marcia, another hitchhiker, (who was a French Canadian) and a huge, yellow dog with mud in his tail. With all of us plus two cases of beer on board we made for the Nevada state line.

The passenger compartment of that truck was close quarters. I had the dog on one knee and Marcia on the other. I must confess that as we rode along I began in my mind to conceive lewd designs on the girl. I must further confess that I acted on those lewd thoughts by placing my left hand on her thigh.

She looked at me square in the eye through her wire-rimmed spectacles and coldly said, "Cool it, Romeo. I'm a lezzie." She then stuck out her tongue which in those close quarters nearly touched the tip of my nose.

We crossed the Bonneville Salt Flats after nightfall, so I really didn't get a good look. The truth is by that time I was so drunk that I really could not have cared less.

It was well after dark when we reached the eastern border of Nevada. There Joe stopped the truck. The Canadian fellow opened the door and we nearly fell out of the truck, reeling from the effects of the alcohol. We thanked Joe and

Marcia, petted the dog, then slammed shut the truck door. We watched as Joe made a U-turn then sped away back toward Salt Lake City.

So there I was, stuck in the middle of nowhere with a guy who couldn't speak English and both of us drunk on our keesters. I slapped him on the back, laughing hysterically. I never did get his name. I just called him "Hey Man!"

From Wendover, Nevada, Hey Man and I hitched a ride to Winnemucca, halfway across the state. At Winnemucca we went into a truck stop. I couldn't believe my eyes! There were gambling devices everywhere!

With hand gestures I told Hey Man that I was going to the men's room. I was really taken aback to find there were even slot machines between the urinals.

I emerged from the wash room just in time to see my French-speaking companion drop a 25-cent piece into a slot machine. He pulled the lever down. The machine clicked several times and then quarters began flowing out of the bottom — hundreds of them!

"Hey Man, ya did it!!" I shouted, running my fingers through the pile of coins on the floor. "Ya hit the jackpot!"

We didn't take the time to count all of that money. With it, though, we feasted on the heartiest steak dinners that place had to offer, laughing at one another the whole time. I think Hey Man was just as hungry as I was.

Our bellies full and for the time being our hearts content we stepped outside the truck stop, picking the leftover steak from between our teeth.

"Here," said Hey Man, holding out two hands full of quarters.

"Naw. That's okay," I said pushing his hands back.

"No. Here. Please," he insisted.

I took the coins and thanked him — and God.

It didn't take us long to get a ride out of Winnemucca. A kind soul in a fancy conversion van gave us a lift as far as Reno, Nevada.

All the way to Reno I stared out of the window into the darkness. I was lost in thought and so hopelessly confused that I again thought of taking my own life.

It was in Reno that Hey Man and I parted company. I took a ride with a trucker and Hey Man took his sleeping bag into some bushes to rest.

By then, Mom, I was quite insane. It is impossible for me to put into words what was going through my mind. The insidiously twisted memories of what were the best moments of my life were being pounded, as if with a hammer, into my consciousness and I was powerless to resist those waves of fiendish assault. I was detached from reality and halfway across the continent from every person, place, or thing I had ever loved.

# VII

# California

Dawn was breaking as the trucker and I wound our way through the mountains of Northern California. The natural beauty was breathtaking. So were the trucker's driving habits. I didn't relax until we were safely on level ground passing through Sacramento.

The sunshine and palm trees were grand. I'd wanted to see California since my early teen years. When I was young it was so glamorized in song. The Mamas & Papas, America, Eric Burden & The Animals, Scott Mackenzie and others had painted such a vivid musical picture of California that I was fascinated by the place.

The way it was portrayed in song I envisioned it as the land of free love, flower power and a haven for drifters such as me.

Since 1967 I had dreamed of seeing California and there it was, unfolding before my very eyes! I nearly wept for joy. "I must also see San Francisco," I silently resolved. That is a dream which I have yet to realize. Yes, I will see San Francisco with my family at my side. But at that time it was not to be. I had set my heart to go to Burbank and to Burbank I would go!

The trucker let me out on Interstate 5 near Stockton. I was immediately a subject of intense interest to a pair of California State Troopers. They came on like gangbusters in separate cruisers sliding to a stop in a cloud of gray dust. As they somewhat hurriedly exited the patrol cars I just stood there smiling. The two swaggered up to me and stood at arm's length.

"Do you have any identification?" asked the taller of the two.

I took my Ohio driver's license out of my shoe and handed it to him. He examined it for a moment.

"You're a long way from home," he said. "What is your destination?"

"Burbank," I replied. "Gonna see my sister."

The trooper gave me back my license as the other one said, "Let me give you some advice. Don't go near Bakersfield or Barstow. All right?"

"Whatever you say," I said.

Before I had a chance to ask the reason behind such a stern warning the troopers returned each to his own vehicle and departed my presence much in the same way they had arrived.

I was suddenly hot. I took off the sweater. I felt weak and feverish. I could hardly stand. I took a few labored steps. My feet felt as heavy as concrete blocks. "I have to go on," I told myself out loud. "I have to get to Burbank. I *have* to!"

Mom, would it hurt you if I revealed why I so desperately needed to get to Burbank? Would it keep you awake tonight if I were to tell you how twisted my thought processes had become?

I will tell you, but not for the sake of heaping sorrow upon sorrow. God knows I have already grieved your soul enough over the years. I will tell you only so you can praise God every day for the rest of your life that I survived and now have my mind restored.

The Apostle Paul wrote to young Timothy that God has not given us a spirit of cowardice, but of power, love and a sound mind (2 Timothy 1:7). These three God has promised through his infallible word to every believer. Even though I do now have some bad times, this promise is to me. For we walk by faith, not by sight (2 Corinthians 5:7). Think on those two scriptures and you find it much easier to keep in mind that I am writing about the "then" in the "now."

You see, I believed actress Angie Dickinson to be my half-sister. In my perverse thinking mode she, my ex-wife and I were the illegitimate children of the late John F. Kennedy. Angie's mother was a lady of the evening, my ex-wife's mother was the late Marilyn Monroe (remember that Marilyn Monroe's real name was Norma Jean. Isn't that name very close to my ex-wife's?), and I was yours. The Kennedys placed me with you and Bob, knowing that I would be reared in a wholesome atmosphere.

I also believed Bob and my natural father, Gale Holbrook, to have been among JFK's personal bodyguards prior to my birth. The deal was that I would carry the Holbrook name and Bob would raise me. He picked out his two best men for the job.

I had many false and contorted memories to back up these delusions which are much too complex to begin to explain. To my depraved way of thinking though, all the pieces fit together very well. I was convinced that fantasy was indeed fact.

There is more. I was convinced that I wrote the lyrics to every song Barry Manilow ever recorded, as well as many songs by rock artists such as Aerosmith, Bob Seger, The Eagles, plus some others. That's why I sent Mr. Manilow that idiotic telegram when I lived in Syracuse, Indiana.

There is still more. I believed there were young men all over the country who were imitating me. (I called them fakers.) They were doing their level best, by conducting themselves like me, dressing like me and mocking my mannerisms, to be mistaken for the mystery songwriter to whom such injustice had been done. I found their antics to be very irritating.

I imagined them accepting money, recognition, lavish gifts and female companionship which rightfully belonged to me. I believed in my heart if I persevered I would get everything that was rightfully mine, marry Patty Hearst, and live happily ever after.

I kept looking and, yes, praying for that golden day. I was reaching, grasping, and holding on as best I could until that glorious morning after. That morning after came on August 18, 1979 — my second wedding day.

I had many more delusions about my circumstances, my past, old friends and relatives than I can possibly describe. To

39

even attempt to explain it all would be reaching far beyond my ability. You know enough to understand that I was quite brain sick.

All of this sounds like a sinister plot doesn't it? In fact there was a conspiracy, but not one perpetrated by any Hollywood celebrity or the FBI. This master plan was conceived and orchestrated by Satan himself and his orders were carried out by an army of demons.

You see, there is a spiritual dimension to mental illness the doctors never dreamed to exist. They really have no idea what they are up against. They can treat symptoms, often successfully, with medications and therapy. I have seen doctors do a great deal of good for a good many people.

Medications can work wonders, but the root cause of every type of mental illness is demonic oppression or possession. It may manifest itself as a chemical imbalance in the brain and often responds to medication, but be assured the devil is at the bottom of it. Doctors can treat symptoms but there will be no permanent progress made until the spiritual aspect of the illness is dealt with. Jesus often healed those who were lunatic by casting out demons.

It is the intent of the devil to cause as much pain to mankind as he possibly can. Believe me, he can really do a number on a mind which has been weakened by drugs and/or alcohol. I know. I have lived that nightmare. I have been there.

Even now I sometimes feel as though there are fakers who have been sent my way to bother me. I have learned, though, that what I am feeling more often than not bears no resemblance to reality. The devil is a liar. Every time his lips move, he is lying. He lies to me every minute of every day.

I'm sure by now you realize there was a mental basket case on his way to see Angie Dickinson. She had enough clout to at least get me my money. She and Johnny Carson would then reveal to the world just who it was who wrote all those great song lyrics.

I gleefully imagined that all fakers would be shot on sight, gunned down in the streets or made to wander with no certain dwelling place, as I was doing, because no one would give them jobs or take them in. They would be hated throughout the whole world for my name's sake! I would then be exalted and recognized for the genius that I was!

These delusions were all I had to go on. They gave me a purpose and a mission. They gave me hope. Without them I most certainly would have done away with myself.

Anyway, I was once again standing along the side of the road with my thumb extended. Vehicles of every description whizzed by. A van came along and slowed as if the driver was contemplating giving me a ride. The van then accelerated rapidly and the driver displayed an obscene gesture. I broke down and wept. I wept because I couldn't fathom such cruelty and because I thought everyone in California knew about and loved me.

At long last I got a ride in a Volkswagen Beetle with a medical student, (whom I presumed to be the older brother of young actress Kristy McNichol). He was an odd sort of person who was wearing large gray ear muffs which he said were to protect his ears from the engine noise. He was returning, supposedly, from a camping trip in the mountains.

After we had ridden along for a few miles he asked if I was hungry. I told him I was, shouting so as to be heard over the drone of the engine and through the ridiculous looking ear muffs. He reached into the back seat and produced a large bag of sunflower seeds which I devoured within the space of eight minutes.

The young student allowed me to ride from Stockton all the way to Los Angeles. As we rode along I got my first look at the desert floor and the mountains surrounding the central valley. I saw the golden sun shining down upon the seemingly endless rows of produce which would eventually find their way to grocery stores perhaps a thousand miles away. The rock group America recorded a song titled "Ventura Highway" which can not be understood by anyone who has never been to southern California.

California. It was far more picturesque than I'd ever imagined.

41

# VIII
## NBC

It was late afternoon when we arrived in Los Angeles. The gregarious scholar treated me to an authentic Mexican dinner in an outdoor cafe and then gave me a mini-tour of the city. We went near an area inhabited almost exclusively by people of Spanish descent. As we turned a corner a Mexican-American teenager looked on us with seething hatred, the likes of which I've never seen before or since.

"We had best get out of here," said my host. "I'm only half Spanish and you are white. If we go any further we may not come out alive."

With that, he abruptly made a tight U-turn with that little car and we went out of the neighborhood the same way we had gone in.

After that, he took me to the railway station and we walked inside together. I recognized the fact that he was trying to give me the slip in there but I kept him in sight and caught up with him outside.

"All right," he said in disgust. "Where do you want to go?"

"Burbank," I said. "NBC studios."

The disgruntlement on his face and in his voice was mounting. "Fine," said my then-reluctant comrade. "Get in."

It was dark when we arrived at NBC studios. In the parking lot I started to get out of the car.

"Wait," the young student said, taking hold of my left forearm. He scribbled a telephone number on a scrap of paper and handed it to me.

"Here's my number," he said. "Call me if anything terrible happens."

I thanked him, shook his hand and got out of the car.

While walking across the parking lot I could hear Doc Severenson and his orchestra playing that familiar *Tonight Show* theme.

Once inside the double glass doors I approached a large counter. A uniformed guard was sitting on the other side reading a newspaper.

"I ... I want to see Mr. Carson," I stammered.

"Can't see him," mumbled the guard without looking up. "He's doing his show." He looked up from his newspaper. "Who are you, anyway?" he asked, getting to his feet.

"Never mind that!" I snapped. "Is Angie Dickinson here?"

"No," said the guard. "She works at Warner Brothers up the street. Who *are* you?"

"I'm Angie's little brother and I demand to see her!"

"You are not anybody! You are a *bum!*" The guard leaned over the counter, his nose inches from mine. "Now," he said in a low, controlled voice, "if you don't leave I'll call the city police and they will make sure you leave. Savvy?"

"Yeah. Yeah," I said. "I'll go but can I make a phone call first?"

"Sure," said the guard leaning back on his heels. "There's a pay phone right over there.

I went to the telephone and reached into my pocket. I still had some of the coins which Hey Man had blessed me with. Along with them I pulled out that tiny scrap of paper that the fellow in the Volkswagen had given me. I could hardly read the numbers, but I deciphered them as best I could and dialed the telephone. I was relieved that I wasn't making a toll call.

I heard the telephone ring on the other end. It rang once ... twice ... three times. I was about to hang up when someone who was obviously intoxicated answered.

"Hello ... Hello!" I shouted into the telephone receiver. "Are you the guy in the Volkswagen that gave me a ride a while ago?"

"What?" shouted a masculine voice on the other end. "No! Never heard of him! Or you!"

"Listen to me! Something terrible has happened!"

"That's not my problem. What did you say your name was?" he said.

"A guy in a Volkswagen told me to call this number if anything terrible happened, so I'm callin'." I could hear people laughing in the background.

"You're crazy! Why don't you call the cops?" shouted the man and then he hung up.

I have never felt more deflated than I did at that moment. The guard probably thought that I was just another faker.

I was 2000 miles from home with just a few coins and nowhere to sleep. Delirious with fever and with eyes filled with tears I placed the telephone receiver back into its cradle.

"Thanks," I said to the guard. He waved sarcastically as I departed the studio lobby. I found my way to Buena Vista park across the street from the studio and sat down at a picnic table to think the situation over.

I sat at the picnic table teary-eyed for a time before I noticed a large building some distance away. Through the trees I could see the brightly lit windows and surmised that it was probably a hospital. I left the park and set out for that place, seeking refuge from the turmoil in my mind and heart.

As I drew near to the structure I discovered my hunch was correct. It was a hospital. I located the emergency room and walked up to the glass window. I pecked on it with a dirty fingernail.

A pretty lady in a nurse's uniform slid the frosted glass back and sweetly asked if she could help me.

"Does this place have a psych ward?" I wearily asked.

"No," answered the nurse with a tone of genuine concern in her voice. "Is there some problem?" she asked.

"Yeah ... Well ... Kind of," I said in a faltering voice. "I'm a long ways from home and I really need a doctor."

"A psychiatrist?" the nurse asked sweetly.

"Yeah," I answered.

"We can't help you here," said the nurse, "but there is a sanitarium near here. I can help you get there."

"Oh, that's okay." I said. "Just tell me where to find it and I think I can get there on my own."

The kind-hearted nurse gave me directions to the sanitarium. It wasn't a long walk up Alameda Avenue to get there, so I arrived in about 20 minutes.

The sanitarium was a lightly colored brick, one-story building with no windows that I could see. There was a metal plaque near the door which read Ring Bell For Assistance. I walked up the concrete steps and extended my grimy right hand to ring the bell.

"*No!!*" I screamed at myself and jerked my hand back. "They'd think I was just another faker, a nut!"

I left that place and paced the distance back to Buena Vista park. I sat down at the same picnic table where I'd been earlier, laid my head to rest, folded my hands and fell fast asleep.

The next thing I knew, I was being awakened by someone shouting, "Hey! Hey!" I awoke with a start and sat bolt upright. My eyes wearily focused upon two men. I stared at them vacantly for ten full seconds before I recognized them as police officers.

"Wake UP!" shouted one of the officers.

"I'm awake! I'm awake already!" I shouted back.

"Got any identification?" asked one of the policemen.

"Yeah. Yeah. Right here," I said still half asleep and disgusted. I took my driver's license from my shoe and handed it to them.

They took a good, long look at my license, nodded to one another, then informed me that I was being taken into custody.

"Aint you gonna read my rights?" I asked as I was being frisked and handcuffed.

"You are not under arrest," said one of the policemen as I was being led away to the patrol car.

After about ten minutes we arrived at the police station. I was placed alone in a cell and given sheets and a pillow case with which to make the bed. I was thinking that jail wasn't going to be so bad after all. I had not so much as seen a real bed in quite some time, much less slept in one.

The next morning I was given breakfast in my cell, my first meal in two days, and asked if I wanted a shower. Of course, I wanted to take a shower. At that time I couldn't have smelled much like Grandma Grunt's rose garden.

There was no hot water in the shower, so I settled for a cold one. After I had dressed, the officers released me and told me where I could find at least a day's work. I worked hard that day and by late afternoon I had a check in my hand worth 30 dollars.

I cashed the check at a bank in the same beautiful downtown Burbank which Dan Rowan and Dick Martin had made famous. I bought some food from a street vendor and a black and white satchel in a nearby drug store. I still have that satchel and wherever I travel it goes with me.

I boarded a city bus and rode it into North Hollywood where I called home. Bob answered the telephone and as calmly as he could asked where and how I was. He made a suggestion which had never crossed my mind. He asked if I could get to Phoenix. I told him I probably could, seeing as how I'd made it to California.

As you know, Bob has an older sister who lives in Phoenix and he asked if I would go there. I thought it was a great idea. It wouldn't be home, but at least I would be among kin folk. I agreed to go on to Phoenix.

Bob insisted on sending me money, so he had 30 dollars sent to a nearby Western Union office. From there I took a taxi to a freeway near Hollywood Boulevard and I was on my way to Arizona.

# IX

# On To Phoenix

It was well after nightfall when I departed from Los Angeles and it took several rides to get me out of the area. I told every driver with whom I rode that Phoenix was my destination and trusted them to let me off at the right places. I was feeling better then, both physically and emotionally. I hadn't encountered any fakers since the night before.

With the help of a man in a Toyota pickup truck I found myself in Indio, California, in the middle of the night. I had made a mistake by taking a ride off of the freeway, which took a path around Indio, and went by way of a two-lane road into the town.

After I got out of the small truck I could see the lights of the Interstate 10 interchange about a mile away across the dark desert. I decided to take a break and get some coffee and a sandwich at an all-night cafe.

As I was sipping on my coffee I came up with an idea. I bought a felt-tipped marker and then rummaged through a garbage dumpster until I found a piece of white cardboard. On it I printed in bold letters the word PHEONIX and set out through the darkness to the freeway interchange.

On the desert it was pitch-black. The only way I could discern that I was still on the narrow pavement was the sound of my heel beat on the asphalt. I was feeling a little jittery. In the distance I could hear the lonesome howl of a dog, or perhaps it was a coyote. The sound sent chills down my spine. I had never been on the desert at all, much less alone in the middle of the night.

At long last I reached the freeway. I got a ride in a van with a man who was very stoned. He was a good driver in spite of his degree of intoxication and I rode with him the remainder of the night.

Just before daybreak he let me off in a tiny place called Desert Center, California. It was there for the first time I beheld the beauty of a desert sunrise.

As I looked across the pale desert sand I saw the huge rocks, mountains as it were, rising like huge monuments off the desert floor. At first they were a hue of purple. As the sun rose just above the horizon they changed color slowly, almost imperceptibly, to a shade of red, and then orange. They seemed to be so close, as though I could reach out and touch them, but I knew they were perhaps miles away.

As I stood awe-struck, I could easily have been persuaded that I was viewing a moonscape. A few minutes later the hot desert sun was up and the rough rocks were a rich bronze color and sparkled as if studded with tiny diamonds.

My consideration of that auroral display was interrupted by the driver of a semi-truck who was parked nearby. I turned as I heard him call to me.

"You want a ride?" he called.

"You bet I do!" I exclaimed and turned to take one final look at the sparkling rocks before I ran to the truck.

Once under way, the driver pulled his cowboy hat down on his brow and said, "I saw you back at Indio last night. But I couldn't stop this whole rig just to pick you up."

He took a sidelong look at me, then chuckled. "By the way, you spelled Phoenix wrong. You look a little tired. Why don't you crawl into the bunk and get some rest."

"Yeah, I am beat. Thanks for the lift," I said, wasting no time in getting into the sleeping compartment of the truck.

The bunk was less than comfortable, but with the drone of the truck's diesel engine below me I soon fell fast asleep.

I don't know how long I slept in the truck, but when I awoke the truck was parked and the cowboy driver was nowhere to be seen.

I bounded out of the truck and looked around me. What I saw was a sort of an archway over the highway. There were vehicles passing under the arch. It appeared to be a check point of some kind.

"The Mexican border!" I exclaimed. Near panic, I ran to the arch and was met by the driver.

"Why did you bring me *here*?" I bellowed. "You knew I wanted to get to Phoenix!"

"What are you talkin' about?" asked the driver. "This is the Arizona state line! I had to stop here and tell 'em what I got on the truck!"

"I'm sorry. I really am. I thought you were takin' me to Mexico." I hung my head.

"Aw, that's all right," said the driver. "C'mon. We've got truckin' to do."

We got back on the road and within a few hours we were on the outskirts of Phoenix. My trucker friend let me off on what I later learned was Buckeye Road. I went into a little farm market, called Aunt Thelma and bought a Coca-Cola. Aunt Thelma said it would be a little while before she could come pick me up, so I went outside to wait.

It was nearly an hour before I saw Aunt Thelma's white Ford coming up the road. I exchanged hellos with her and cousin Mary Ann. They both commented on the fact that I didn't look good. On the road I had contracted a case of the flu.

After we arrived at Aunt Thelma's house she cooked me a good meal of ham and eggs. I never did like to eat eggs, but I was so hungry that I devoured the last morsel.

I hadn't been there long before I rightly judged Aunt Thelma as being an austere, but kindly woman who was deeply concerned about me. I didn't realize it at the time, but cousin Mary Ann was to become my best friend.

We went many places together my first few weeks in Phoenix. We attended concerts at the Arizona State Fair and she treated me to a Mexican dinner. My hostesses gave me the best room in the house. I was regarded as an honored guest and not the madman I later revealed myself to be.

# X
# From Bad To Worse

Within a few weeks of my arrival in Phoenix I had taken to drinking excessively. My favorite bar was a place called La Pinata, the same Mexican restaurant where Mary Ann and I often dined. I often left that place nearly too intoxicated to walk the nine or so blocks home.

One evening at La Pinata I met up with a pretty blonde lady who was a few years my senior, but nonetheless attractive. She invited me to a place up 19th Avenue near Indian School Road called the Paradise Tavern. That place became my usual hangout.

The blonde and I began seeing each other, but she had more hang-ups than the local dry cleaners. At that time I needed someone who could help me get straight, not confuse me even more.

It seemed I visited the Paradise Tavern nearly every evening and became very well acquainted with the owners.

I fancied myself as being a tough guy and soon became the self-appointed bouncer of the tavern. That was a dangerous position for me to be in, taking into consideration my shortness of stature. I consider it a miracle that I didn't get the daylights beaten out of me, because I was quite a cocky little fellow.

My behavior, which often frightened and confused Mary Ann, and my episodes of drunkenness were steadily growing more extreme. I felt as though I had become a burdensome disruption to Aunt Thelma's household. So I set about to find my own place where I could carry on my demented lifestyle without disturbing anyone else.

I soon moved into a small apartment directly across 19th Avenue from the Paradise Tavern. On most nights I would stagger across 19th Avenue in a drunken stupor, fall into bed and cry a cry from the depths of my soul. My feelings could not be expressed in mere words, but alone at night they would come out in a gush of tears and moanings which no one else saw or heard.

I was so far from home. I had no meaningful relationships. Probably that was because I hid behind my bottle and my psychotic behavior and wouldn't allow anyone to give me what I needed most, which was love. I had no real friends and those who would associate with me were so taken aback by my behavior they sometimes shunned me because there was no telling what I would say or do next.

About that time a new delusion began to force its way into my consciousness. I believed that as a child I was placed under hypnosis and left with a post-hypnotic suggestion.

That suggestion was that when I heard the words, "go under," I would immediately lapse into a trance and was at the mercy of the person who had put me "under." Then when I heard the words, "come out," I would be myself again and have no recollection of what had transpired while I was in that hypnotic state.

All of this was common knowledge in Phoenix and everywhere I went people were putting me under and bringing me out according to their pleasure. This included that army of fakers who dogged my steps daily. This was my way of explaining the lapses in memory I was experiencing.

I was among men most miserable. I made it a point only to associate with the few persons I thought I could trust, which included the owners of the Paradise Tavern and their daughter.

Within were fears, abstract thoughts and the lust for alcohol. Without were fakers at every hand and a city of one million people, any one of whom could at will put me in a hypnotic trance.

I was lost, lost in life. Every stranger's face I saw and every faker I encountered only served to intensify that feeling. I had lost the hope that I would some day rise above all the mess, be vindicated and recognized as a brilliant songwriter.

I was being buried alive in an avalanche of deception, unspeakable malice and sham. I felt that I had become the most hated person since Adolf Hitler. My every action and word was being scrutinized.

All eyes were upon me. I had no place to hide, no place of refuge. Even my apartment was under electronic surveillance. I had become weary in mind, soul and spirit.

All of this bombarded me day and night until one evening, in a fit of despair, I swallowed half a bottle of extra-strength Tylenol with several cups of black coffee. I laid down on my bed and silently waited for death to overtake me.

I was semi-conscious for a time until fear overwhelmed me. If I was to succeed in committing suicide I would forever be reserving for myself a place in hell with no time off for good behavior.

The thought of all that was too much for me to bear and I jerked myself off my bed and unsteadily made my way to the next apartment.

I knocked on the door. There was no answer. I pounded on the door. The lady who lived there finally answered the door.

"Pat!" I gasped. "Get me a doctor! Hurry!"

My neighbor called the paramedics and they transported me to Phoenix General Hospital which was a few blocks away.

In the emergency room I was forced to drink Ipecac with warm water and immediately began to vomit. The color of the emesis was bright red. An orderly, Mr. Vasquez by name, alerted two doctors who stood nearby.

"Tell me what you had for supper!" Mr. Vasquez demanded.

I refused to answer.

"Tell me what you had to eat!" he shouted as he took me by the shoulders and violently shook my body.

I remained silent.

55

"Unless you really want to die you'll tell me what you had for supper!" The orderly seemed to be growing angry.

"Nothing," I managed to blurt out between violent heaves.

By this time the two doctors had come close. They conferred at length as I was giving a demonstration of classic projectile vomiting. Almost before I knew it I was on my way to the Intensive Care Unit of the hospital. I was to remain there a full week.

After a day or so I was permitted to take sips of water which I immediately threw up along with massive amounts of blood. I continued to sip water until I was able to keep it down. A nurse brought me a Dixie cup full of foul-smelling liquid mixed with Coca-Cola. She said it was for my liver and demanded that I drink it. I have never, before or since, tasted anything so rank. I took one sip and refused to carry the exercise any further.

"If you want to live you'll drink it," said the catty nurse.

"I wanted to die. That was the whole idea," I replied.

"Suit yourself," she said, then walked away.

I drank it. All of it. Not only that cupful, but six per day.

Two Phoenix city policemen visited me in the hospital. They wanted to question me because they keep records on suicide attempts. I was just another statistic.

After seven full days at Phoenix General I was pronounced well enough to travel across town to the Veterans Administration Hospital. I was admitted to the psychiatric unit there and spent some time getting acquainted with the fellow patients and staff, all the while on guard for possible fakers.

Later that evening as the others were busy in the game room or watching television I went alone into the huge, darkened dining room. I sat at a table far from the door and began to sob uncontrollably. I wept long and hard with my face pressed against the table.

I thought a suicide attempt would evoke pity in the hearts of my persecutors, who were standing between me and my rightful place in Hollywood. But there seemed to be no pity and no way out of the hellish nightmare in which I was living. "After all the songs ..." I wailed. "After all the good T.V. shows ..." I sobbed. "Why won't those fakers stop? ... I can't take any more! ... I can't! ... I can't! Oh, God! ... Why, God? ... What did I do?"

I wept there alone in the semi-darkness for the better part of an hour before I looked up. There on the table beside me was a neatly folded clean towel. Someone had slipped in and placed it there without my being aware of it.

I stopped crying, dried my eyes and blew my nose. Through the sobbing I had rekindled what sanity had been lying dormant within me. I felt restored, renewed and ready to carry on. In that hour I had cried out of my being all the loneliness, fear, confusion and frustration which I had held inside. I slept well that night. It was a dreamless, blissful, peaceful sleep which everyone needs and I had not had in months.

On my third day at the hospital I was summoned to the doctor's office. The psychiatrist was a rather young man who sported a beard. He had more the appearance of a jazz musician than a doctor. He was a rather quiet but compassionate soul. We talked for about half an hour and in that time I conned him into letting me out of the hospital.

My lunacy had for the moment abated and there was no real reason that I could see to justify my being in the hospital any longer.

Mary Ann came to visit me that day and was flabbergasted to learn that I had been released. I begged her not to call Aunt Thelma so the two of them could have me committed. I feared that, because I had bad experiences with doctors and hospitals.

As Mary Ann placed a call to Aunt Thelma I begged not to be committed. The pleading paid off and I was permitted to leave with Mary Ann.

I returned to my apartment and found that while I was ill someone had ransacked it. The building manager informed me that I was being evicted and assessed damages to the place. I had no place to go, so long-suffering Mary Ann and Aunt Thelma took me in once more.

# XI

# My Freedom Machine

It was about that time Aunt Thelma decided that having an automobile would really be good for me. So she, Mary Ann, and I went car shopping.

We visited a few lots before we happened upon a cute little yellow Volkswagen Beetle. Aunt Thelma offered to furnish the down payment and co-sign for the loan, but I balked. I felt as if I had already imposed upon her enough and secretly wondered if I would keep up the payments.

I couldn't allow her to stick her neck out for me. She had already bought me clothing, housed me and fed me at great personal expense. That is not to mention putting up with my maniacal behavior. I had tried to repay her with cash and performing chores around the house, but I always felt as though I was coming up short.

About a week after that on one of my many long walks I happened upon a motorcycle which was for sale. The seller, I discovered, was a Phoenix city police officer. The price was right so I bought the motorcycle and after a few relatively minor repairs the little beast was street-worthy.

It was only a little 250cc trail or street bike but it got me around. I rode it everywhere. I would leave early in the morning and return late at night.

I rode through the beautiful Superstition Mountains, out through Cave Creek Canyon and up the Black Canyon freeway. I often rode to Encanto Park at daybreak to feed morsels of bread to the ducks and geese.

I explored the city and country on that little two-wheeler. Every nook and cranny of the mountains around Phoenix and even Apache Junction were my stomping grounds as long as I had my wheels beneath me.

I rode across the hot, arid desert and into the cold of Flagstaff, often leaving the paved road for the fun of trail riding in no man's land. I loved my freedom machine.

Not far from where Aunt Thelma lived was a church which operated a private school. I liked to ride past that place, downshift into a low gear, let out the clutch and chuckle as the popping and cracking of my unbaffled muffler disturbed classes.

I was riding past that church one Sunday evening, my engine roaring as usual, just as services were being dismissed. There was a group of young people standing out in front and as I came by they called to me.

"Hey, you! C'mere!" shouted one of the young men.

I supposed he was looking for a fight, which I was obliged to give him. Being the macho man that I was, I steered the motorcycle onto the sidewalk, applied the rear brake, turned the front wheel and slid sideways to a stop.

"What do ya want?" I said as arrogantly I could. A tall girl with long, dark hair walked up to me.

"We've been waiting to meet you," she said. "We were going out for pizza. Would you like to come along?"

"Really?" I asked in disbelief.

"Yes," she said. "Won't you please join us?"

She was taller than I, but her gentle eyes and silky, shoulder-length hair were enchanting. Her smile disarmed me.

"I can't go like this," I said referring to my dingy jeans, jacket and boots.

The girl smiled again and said, "Sure you can. We'd love to have you as our guest."

I shut down the noisy motorcycle engine and dismounted.

"Real Christians!" I thought to myself. "They don't care how I look or act. They like me anyway!"

Actually, what I had hoped for was taking place. I was longing for a lovely, young girl and her friends to cut through the facade and sham of the untouchable, little tough guy.

Inside of me was a lonely man yearning for love. Inside of me was beating a bruised and bleeding heart.

Someone had at last seen through me and sensed my need to be loved and accepted just for whom and what I was, not what others thought I should be.

We went to a large Italian restaurant. They were, as Christian young people go, a rather rowdy group. Sandy, as she told me her name was, kept staring across the table at me, a wistful smile upon her lips. I avoided all eye contact. I felt hot and cold at the same time. My deodorant had worn off and I kept having to wipe my brow.

As we talked I learned that Sandy's parents were missionaries and that she was a freshman at a Bible college in another state. She said she would be in Phoenix only for a short time.

The evening ended too soon. Back at the church, I promised I'd be her pen pal. She waved as I kick-started my motorcycle and sped away into the darkness.

Not long after that night I was riding through Cave Creek Canyon late in the evening. I was enjoying the freedom and exhilaration which comes with riding on the open road when on old Chevy full of teenagers passed me at a high rate of speed. I saw a pistol hang out the right rear window. Then I saw a muzzle flash. I applied my rear brake hard and slid to a stop. I realized that I had nearly been shot.

Another day I was riding in the mountains north of Phoenix, coming down from a higher elevation. I laid out flat on my fuel tank so as to cut wind resistance and obtain maximum speed.

My speedometer read 60 ... then 65 ... 70 ... 72. I decided that was enough and let off the throttle. I sat upright on the seat and spied one of the many gravel lanes along side of the road. I locked up my rear brake and slid to a stop in a cloud of dust.

I removed my helmet and dismounted. I walked to the edge of the cliff and looked down. I surmised that it was at least 600 feet to the bottom of the canyon. I then looked at my motorcycle. It was parked less than six feet from the edge of the cliff. It dawned on me that I had nearly ridden off a cliff.

I do believe in guardian angels, Mom, and I kept mine busy.

# XII

# The Assassin

---

One night at the Paradise Tavern I was minding my own business, which was guzzling beer with the owner's daughter, when I was suddenly surrounded by a group of uniformed men — all members of the local constabulary. I recognized one of them as the man from whom I bought my motorcycle and directed an inquiry to him.

"Hey, fellas. Whatziz all about?" I asked as plainly as I could, for I was quite drunk.

"How much have you had to drink?" asked another of the cops.

"'Nuff," I replied, taking another gulp of beer.

"How do you feel about Gerald Ford?" asked another.

"Gerry Ford!" I bellowed. "My Gawd! Gerald Ford! I think I voted for him. Whatziz all about anyhow?"

"Then you like him?" asked one of the policemen.

"Well, if I didden like the guy I wouldn't have voted for him would I?"

"Okay," said the cop who was the former owner of my freedom machine. He then added, "Stay close for a few days. Okay, Adam?"

"Surely as you speak," I said after a short, muffled beer belch.

"Are you planning on riding your motorcycle home?" asked still another of the policemen.

"Certainly not!" I replied after another gulp of brew. "I'm gonna walk. I am in no condition to be operating a (hic!) motor vehicle."

With that, the police left.

The next evening, by way of the KTAR television news, I learned that former president Gerald Ford was visiting Phoenix to play in a golf tournament.

"How do ya like that?" I said. "They think I'm a bloomin' assassin!"

"What?" said Mary Ann as I stomped out of the room.

Later that night I packed a few belongings in my satchel and left for California. I was going to put a stop to all of this nonsense once and for all.

Two days later, as I arrived at NBC studios, fear gripped my heart. My reason for making the long trip there was to straighten out the whole mess other people had made of my life and get the fakers off my back. But, an attack of sheer panic kept me in the parking lot. I turned away, disgusted with myself for having come such a long way for nothing. I swore at myself all the way back to the Golden State Freeway.

On my way back to Phoenix after my aborted mission of self-liberation, I was given a ride in the early afternoon by two guys in an ancient Chevrolet. They picked me up on the outskirts of Los Angeles. The two men were soft-spoken, solemn hippies.

Precisely why I don't know, but we wound up in Riverside and later, probably due to a series of wrong turns, in Palm Desert.

At that time the skies were cloudy, much to the delight of the locals because southern California had been experiencing drought conditions for quite some time.

Suddenly the heavens opened and it began to rain. I had never seen rain fall so fast and so hard. Soon the storm drains were backed up and water ran at least a foot deep in the streets.

The water splashed up on the engine of that old car and it stalled. The driver tried in vain to restart it, but it had become water logged. We opened the doors to get out and water gushed into the passenger compartment. We got out of the car and pushed it onto the parking lot of a nearby pharmacy.

By then we were drenched to the bone. After about two hours the rain ended, the storm drains were flowing once again, and our engine dried out enough to be started. We continued on toward Phoenix.

Back in Phoenix a few days later I watched the *Tonight Show* long enough to hear Johnny Carson announce the drought to be officially over. It had rained in Los Angeles for two days.

# XIII

# Return To Burbank

While I was in Phoenix I wrote a lot. Most of these twisted works have been destroyed, but some I sent to celebrities. I wrote lyrics for an entire album and mailed them to the Electric Light Orchestra only to have them refused. On New Year's Day 1978 I wrote a beautiful piece of prose and sent it as a gift to Barry Manilow. I wrote letters to my beloved Angie Dickinson, but she never responded.

I also wrote to Johnny Carson and sent him a color 8 X 10 photograph of Daniel. All he did was make a crude remark on the air which meant nothing to anyone except me. In my demented mind I thought these people were my friends and I just couldn't understand why they wouldn't respond to my personal correspondence.

I was getting messages, so I believed, from the KTAR television nightly news broadcasts. On top of all that, I felt as though I could not go out in public without my every word and movement being scrutinized by the public who could, at will, place me under hypnosis.

Not even my bedroom at Aunt Thelma's house was sacred. I believed there were hidden cameras and microphones in the heating and air conditioning ducts.

Then, of course, I had to deal with that army of ubiquitous fakers who were bent on tormenting me day and night. They wanted me to give up all claims to the fame and fortune which I believed to be rightfully mine.

I'm not certain they would have stopped even if I were to lie and declare myself to be a faker like all of them. I was sure they would continue until I was dead, killed by another faker or by my own hand. I had no choice but to fight.

Still though, there was something which you placed deep inside of me, Mom. It was a powerful, unseen force which kept in check any violent impulse to do harm to another human being.

Within me there was a still, small voice which was ever present and constantly reminding me that what I was experiencing in thought and emotion lacked any semblance of reality. This ember of sanity flared at times and I was able to see things as they really were. But it was all too quickly doused by the demonic powers who were seeking control over my total being.

My soul was weak and weary from the constant internal warfare. I decided to take matters into my own hands once more. I was returning to Burbank one last time.

I rode my motorcycle to Chris-Towne shopping center and there, in the presence of a uniformed city police officer, purchased a handgun. At home I cut pieces from my old suede jacket and sewed a makeshift holster to the inside of my motorcycle jacket.

After Mary Ann and Aunt Thelma were in bed sleeping that night I set out hitchhiking for Burbank packing a gun.

Night had fallen the next evening by the time I arrived at NBC studios. I carried my black and white bag which contained my pistol across the parking lot and stashed it in a row of shrubbery near the entrance.

I was thinking I would try the peaceful approach first and if that failed, I'd come outside and get my gun. One way or another I was going to force the hand of those who had gone to such extremes to keep me from being discovered.

Once inside the lobby I demanded to see Johnny Carson and was immediately ordered off the premises. I left the building grudgingly, swearing under my breath. I went to get my gun.

It was then that still, small voice which had up to then kept me out of trouble began to speak. The unseen and all-knowing Holy Spirit of God constrained me. I came to my senses and realized that a shoot-out with the NBC guard meant a long stay in the hoosegow, a gunshot wound or some worse thing.

I found my bag in the hedgerow and realized I had neglected to get my jacket out of the automobile in which I had arrived. Two men in a green Ford were one imitation leather motorcycle jacket richer. I hope it fits.

When I left NBC I walked up Alameda Avenue toward the Golden State Freeway. Had I invested in a good road map I would have known this was the long way around to where I wanted to go.

As I walked along under the amber street lights I became aware of the sound of music being played at a high decibel level. Perhaps the sound was emanating from a nearby car stereo, but it was nonetheless crystal clear. I recognized the song. It was Diana Ross singing the theme from "Mahogany." "Do you know where you're goin' to? Do you like the things that life is showin' you . . .?"

That haunting melody seemed to have been written just for me and just for that time. As abruptly as the music began, it stopped. I buried my face in my hands and wept until I reached the freeway. There I fell prostrate, face down in the lush vegetation near the ramp as a flood of tears stung my cheeks. I sobbed until no more tears would come.

# XIV

# The Party

After that heart-rending episode I felt weak and a little disoriented but I managed to get to my feet and solicit rides from passersby. Presently a baby blue Cadillac stopped and the driver sounded the horn.

I was no sooner in the car than I reckoned the driver to be a man of means. His expensive automobile and clothing bore immutable witness to his not being a pauper.

As we drove along the Golden State Freeway he told me he was a rock music promoter on his way to a party in San Demas. After a few more miles he asked me if I'd like to go along to the party.

At first I was hesitant, but his coaxing paid off and I agreed to accompany him. I'd always liked partying with musicians. I'd done that as a younger man and I knew it was bound to be a good time.

When we arrived in San Demas my host introduced me to the crowd. They were a rowdy lot and seemed to be having a merry old time. There was plenty of beer and a few people were off in one corner of the living room smoking an infamous herbal intoxicant. Before long I was as drunk as they were and my troubles, at least for that moment, were forgotten.

In the course of the evening I found myself conversing in the kitchen with the very pregnant fiance of one of the musicians. I confessed to her that I was none other than the younger half brother of one Angie Dickinson. Much to my chagrin she burst into a fit of laughter. The more I tried to convince her, the harder she laughed. Finally I decided to keep quiet for fear she would go into labor then and there.

A little while later one of the partyers announced that we were running low on beer. I went to my bag intending to pull out my clock radio which I'd brought along to sell in case I needed to raise money. I thought I would give it to them as a way of paying for my share of the beverages. But when I brought the radio out of my satchel the pregnant girl saw my pistol. She circulated discreetly through the crowd warning all present of my packing a piece.

The men who were going for the drinks refused my offer of the radio, telling me with smiles that the beer was on them.

About that time we decided to watch some television. I was sitting on the sofa watching with the others when two fellows burst through the door.

"There's cops *every*where out there!" exclaimed one.

"Yeah! The neighborhood's crawlin' with 'em!" said the other.

"Must be heavy," said the pregnant girl. "Let's turn on the news."

She quickly changed channels just in time for us to hear the police had released a composite sketch of the then famous Hillside Strangler. What then flashed upon the television screen chilled our blood.

There, in living color, for all to see was a drawing of a person who bore more than a striking resemblance to yours truly. My heart nearly stopped. All present turned and looked upon me. For a full minute stony silence prevailed. I felt the blood drain from my face. Not a word was spoken but their eyes said it all.

Fear, outrage, apprehension, disgust and hatred were in those eyes and all of those eyes were fastened upon me.

After that period of uneasy silence a pretty blonde girl switched off the television set and shrugged her shoulders at the crowd. I was expecting to be physically ejected from the premises, but to my surprise, the ear-splitting music was switched back on. The people went back to chattering as if nothing had happened.

I sat dumbfounded on the sofa until a long-haired man pushed an open Budweiser into my hand and said with a wink of an eye, "Have a beer, man."

Later I was introduced to a man who was supposedly a cousin of the late, great Jimi Hendrix.

"I dig your music," he said as he shook my hand.

"I dig Jimi's too," I said smiling.

That compliment, feigned or otherwise, whether given in jest or sincerity, served to bolster my delusion of being a great songwriter. He was one of the few people who knew of and believed in this creative genius who was being forced to live as an itinerant schizophrenic.

I spent that night on the sofa, fitfully sleeping with my bag serving as a pillow. I know the others who spent the night couldn't have slept well either. How could they with an armed stranger who was suspected of being a serial killer in the next room?

As I stepped outside the next morning I took a good look around. To my relief there were no police. I joined five others in cramming themselves into a Toyota.

"Where'd all the cops go?" said someone as he climbed into the car.

"I dunno," said another. "Just get in."

My hosts were about to let me off at the freeway when someone in the back asked for a roach clip.

"I think I might have a hair pin," I said as I unzipped my satchel.

"He's goin' for it!" came a nearly hysterical voice from the back seat.

"I told you guys we shudda called the cops!" said another.

"Relax," I said, digging through the bag. "No. Crudd! No clip in here," I said as I zipped the bag closed.

Those in the car breathed a sigh of relief as I climbed out. I could hear someone in the car say, "Good riddance." as I closed the door.

The place where they let me off was a little side road. You know, one of those roads that if you stayed on it long enough you'd probably get there. There wasn't much traffic on that road so I had a hard time getting a ride. Another reason could have been that the Hillside Strangler was still on the loose.

Anyway, I was standing along the side of that practically deserted road when I spied a female figure walking toward me. In the distance I could discern she had long brown hair and wore eyeglasses. "Hi," I said as the girl drew near. "You hitchhikin' too?"

"I might have to," she said, smiling. "My car broke down up on the freeway," she said as she pointed to a lone auto sitting on a nearby overpass. "I think the rear end went out, or something."

I immediately suspected her as being an undercover police officer.

"How can I help?" I asked.

"For starters you can stay with me until I can get a ride."

"Okay," I said. "Just sit here on this bag."

The reason I had her sit on the bag was that if she were an undercover cop she would have known there was a gun in the bag. With her sitting on the bag there was no way I could have gotten to the gun. Do you follow me? Therefore, she would feel safe and know I had no evil intent.

We were there for the better part of an hour before a blue pickup truck stopped and the driver gave us a lift to a restaurant.

As we climbed out of the truck the girl pressed a dollar bill into my hand. I tried to refuse the money but she insisted that I take it. She explained (not in so many words) that my presence had served to ward off any malefactors and she was grateful. I tucked the bill in my shirt.

With the usual hitchhiker's stance I solicited rides to Phoenix. I wanted to get back there because I was expecting a letter from Sandy, the girl whom I had met at the church. It was a letter which never came.

# XV

# Closer To Home

A week later I was sitting in the Paradise Tavern drinking with the owner's daughter and made an off-hand remark about needing a hypodermic syringe.

I knew what I wanted. There seemed to be no way I could ever cut through my mental confusion. If Jimi Hendrix' cousin couldn't help me, who on earth could?

Sure I would drink, laugh and have a good time, but in the solitude of my room after the bars closed I would cry a cry that erupted from the depths of my being. My soul was tortured and bleeding and there seemed to be no one or no thing that could erase that pain.

The next evening I strode into the Paradise Tavern and sat down at the bar with the owner's daughter. She suggested we go for a walk. As we strolled up 19th Avenue, she produced from her purse the needle I'd requested the night before.

"Do I owe you for this?" I asked.

"No," she said. "It's a personal favor."

I immediately gave the syringe back to the girl. I had found out what I wanted to know. She was on the side of the fakers and hoped, as they did, that I would use the needle to commit suicide.

I drank more than my fill that night and staggered back to Aunt Thelma's house about 3:00 a.m. I fell into my bed and wept bitterly until daybreak.

I was certain there was no escape from the fakers as long as I remained in Phoenix. I decided to go home. If they wanted me they'd have to chase me down and I was prepared to give them a run for their money.

That day I waited until Aunt Thelma had gone to her job and Mary Ann was out for the day. I packed everything I owned in a trunk and telephoned the Sky Harbor airport to make flight reservations for my journey home. I booked passage on a flight to Dayton which was to depart two days in the future.

I gathered all of my money, which included the proceeds from the sale of my motorcycle, in the trunk and called for a taxi.

The cab arrived at precisely the same time that Mary Ann returned home. As I threw the trunk into the taxi I did my best to ignore her. I was leaving and that was all there was to it!

"Where to?" asked the droll cabby as I slid into the back seat.

"A motel near Sky Harbor," I said.

"Which one?" the driver asked.

"*Any* of them!" I shouted.

"You sure you wanna go?" asked the cabby looking over his shoulder at me.

"*Yes!*" I shouted. "Let's get outa here!"

"Okay! Okay!" replied the driver as he put the cab into gear.

With that we backed out of the drive and sped away. Mary Ann wept as she watched us go.

Within a few minutes we arrived at a motel. I paid the cab fare plus a generous tip. I checked into the motel and stowed my gear in my room.

The next thing I did, Mom, was call you to let you know I was coming home. You'll remember that you told me my sister, Rhonda, was soon to be married. I silently wondered what kind of character she had hooked up with this time. She had done all right by herself I found out later. I couldn't have asked for a better brother-in-law than Bob Mowery.

After I had finished talking with you I set out on foot to explore that part of Phoenix which I had never seen before. I walked past the county hospital where I'd almost been sent when I swallowed all that Tylenol.

76

I was grieved in my heart and spirit because it seemed I had come a long way for nothing. I had come west to claim what fame and fortune was rightfully mine and was going home empty-handed.

While on my walk I hit upon an idea. Why not make one more trip to California? But I wouldn't go as a bum again. Perhaps the stars of Hollywood would accept me if I rented a car and drove to NBC. Maybe then Angie wouldn't be ashamed of me.

With that plan in mind I hurried back to the motel and called a car rental agency listed in the massive Phoenix yellow pages. They sent a driver to the motel to pick me up.

Once at the rental agency I strode in as if I owned the place. While the clerk was filling out the necessary paperwork he asked me for my credit card.

"What credit card?" I asked.

"You don't have a credit card?" asked the clerk with raised eyebrows.

"No ..." I said as my voice began to falter.

"In that case I'll need a deposit of 500 dollars," said the clerk.

"I don't have that either," I said sheepishly. "But," I said, gaining boldness, "if I can get to California my sister will pay the bill. She's rich."

"Just who might your sister be?" asked the clerk as he grew noticeably annoyed.

"Angie Dickinson," I said boastfully. "She'll pay any amount you ask for."

The clerk beckoned to the driver who had picked me up at the motel and said, "Take this gentlemen back to his motel."

It was getting towards evening when I arrived back at the motel. I decided to visit the motel lounge. By the time the live music started I was very well intoxicated.

About that time a somewhat attractive, though chubby, lady took the bar stool next to mine. I sized the lady up in 30 seconds.

"You a pro?" I asked, supposing her to be a prostitute.

"No . . ." she replied being obviously puzzled by my question. She climbed off the bar stool and joined a group of people at a nearby table.

I drank my fill and before midnight I was passed out in my room.

The next day as I emerged from my room onto the sunlit parking lot I spied the lady I had propositioned the night before walking with the biggest human being I'd ever seen. That fellow could have easily passed for a first cousin to the Incredible Hulk.

In stark terror, with my heart pounding, I ducked back inside and locked the door. After a few minutes I peeked out to see if the coast was clear. It was.

I spent the next 14 hours looking over my shoulder to see if that mountain of a man had decided to defend his lady's honor.

That night about seven I dined at the motel restaurant and then went to the lounge for a few drinks. A few drinks became many. By the time I left for the airport at 10:30 I was once again three sheets to the wind.

While checking my luggage at the airport I informed the clerk about the gun in my trunk.

"A gun?" asked the clerk.

"*Yes*, a gun!" I retorted. "It is *un*loaded and it is taken apart into teeny, tiny little pieces."

"Oh," said the clerk looking at her computer screen. "You must be Mr. Holbrook."

"The gun will be fine," she said smiling.

"Thanks," I said and then made my way to the lounge.

I staggered in and sat down at the bar next to a man dressed in a business suit. I ordered a rum and Coke and proceeded to engage the man in a conversation concerning how well then-president Jimmy Carter was running the country.

Have you ever sat sober and listened to drunk people discuss politics? It is disgusting. I pray the other patrons were too engrossed in their own things to pay us any mind.

Some think it impossible to drink oneself sober, but that is what I did that night. By the time I left the lounge I was not feeling the least bit drunk, but extremely fatigued.

I left the lounge and proceeded to a snack bar where I bought myself a sandwich and a soft drink. I found myself surrounded not by fakers, but men in business suits. It is not uncommon to see men dressed in that way at airports. But their presence disturbed me.

I felt as though I was surrounded by FBI agents. I wolfed down the sandwich in time to board my plane.

A few minutes later I was on that eastbound airplane, with seat belt securely fastened, as it ascended high above the earth.

It was an incredibly clear night and I beheld the lights of the city below me. I tearfully waved goodbye to Phoenix and remembered all the people I had met there. I recalled all of the bad times as well as the few good times. I didn't know for certain if I would ever return, but I knew I would never forget what had happened there.

I ordered a cup of coffee from the flight attendant and stared out the window into the darkness. I studied the clusters of light below me and the bright stars above.

I wondered about my future, where I would go, and what I would find when I got home. I wondered also if all those fakers would follow me and if they'd ever give up their relentless pursuit of my sanity.

I thought of home, the farm, the house, and all my old friends and relatives who had made my life so full in previous years. Would they be there? Would they understand? Would they still love me?

I was dazed and confused but I was going home. I was going back to my roots. I was going back to the people who had helped bring about every good and wholesome experience I'd ever known. I was going home . . .

The date was February 8, 1978.

Well, Mom, you know the rest of the story. It all worked out for God's glory, even though there were moments when I know you'd have just as soon let me rot in whatever institution I happened to be.

79

When you think of me now with my beautiful wife and family, when you think of how I have found my place in our great society, when you think of how gracious and merciful God has been to me, it is then the time to thank Jesus Christ, the author and finisher of our faith. It is only by God's unending love, grace and mercy that I am what I am.

Praise God in heaven forevermore!

I love you.

Your son,
Adam